& HIS SIX WIVES

JOHN GUY

for Ann

snapping-turtle
guide

THE YOUNG
HENRY

*H*enry came to the throne at the age of 17, a handsome, robust giant of a man standing 6ft (1.83metres) tall, when the average height was just 5ft. 4ins (1.6metres). He had not been groomed for kingship and lacked the necessary discipline to rule responsibly. A flamboyant character, he squandered his father's fortune and was more interested in sports, music and dancing than in politics, leaving policy-making decisions to a group of astutely chosen ministers.

CEREMONIAL ARMOUR

This finely silvered and engraved suit of armour was made for Henry. It was used mostly for parading during tournaments.

THE THRILL OF THE HUNT

Henry loved to hunt in the forests attached to the royal palaces, particularly with birds of prey. There was a strict hierarchy to be observed, kestrels such as this were flown by lesser nobles, or Henry himself when learning his skills. Later, he would probably have flown a larger species, such as the Peregrine falcon or an eagle.

HENRY VIII

This portrait miniature shows Prince Henry as a young boy. The third child (and second son) of Henry VII, he was not born to rule and only came to the throne as the result of his brother Arthur's untimely death in 1502.

HENRY VII

Henry Tudor was born at Pembroke Castle in 1457. An only child, his mother was the great-great-granddaughter of Edward III. He spent 14 years in exile before being crowned king at the age of 28, beginning the reign of the Tudors.

EVENTS OF HENRY'S LIFE

~1485 22ND AUGUST~
Battle of Bosworth Field

~29TH OCTOBER~
Henry VII crowned

16TH DECEMBER
Catherine of Aragon born

~1486~
Prince Arthur born

~1491 28TH JUNE~
Prince Henry (later Henry VIII) born

~1501 14TH NOVEMBER~
Marriage of Prince Arthur and Catherine of Aragon

~1502~
Prince Arthur dies. Anne Boleyn born

THE TUDORS COME TO POWER

Henry Tudor wrested the crown by defeating the Plantagenet king, Richard III, at the Battle of Bosworth on 22nd August 1485. Civil war (the Wars of the Roses) had raged for over 30 years between two rival claimants to the throne - the House of York (Richard) and the House of Lancaster (Henry).

THE GOLDEN YEARS

The 'Golden Years' of Henry's reign coincided with his marriage to Catherine of Aragon. He married the last five of his wives and committed most of his acts of tyranny within the last third of his reign. When he ascended the throne as a robust, gallant teenager, he was welcomed. The people rejoiced as the years of restraint under Henry VII ended. Henry VIII appeared to promise much, but he did not live up to their expectations.

THE KING'S DEPARTURE

The scene at Dover, May 1520, when Henry and his court of 5,800 embarked for their meeting with the King of France.

THE 'UNKNOWN WARRIOR'

Henry was very proficient at jousting. He sometimes fought as an unknown contender, only to later reveal his true identity as the victor to the jubilant crowds, who no doubt pretended to be fooled!

THE KING'S GREAT MATTER

Henry blamed Catherine's inability to conceive a son and heir on God's punishment for marrying his brother's widow. He tried to have the marriage annulled on the grounds that it was unlawful, so he could remarry.

COUNTRY RETREAT

The Tudor banqueting hall of Leeds Castle, Kent. Henry built a fine suite of royal apartments here for use when he wished to escape the ills of London.

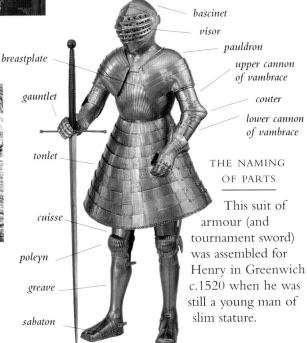

- bascinet
- visor
- pauldron
- upper cannon of vambrace
- breastplate
- gauntlet
- couter
- lower cannon of vambrace
- tonlet
- cuisse
- poleyn
- greave
- sabaton

THE NAMING OF PARTS

This suit of armour (and tournament sword) was assembled for Henry in Greenwich c.1520 when he was still a young man of slim stature.

CATHERINE OF ARAGON

BORN
1485

MARRIED
1509

DIVORCED
1533

DIED
1536

Catherine was the only child of King Ferdinand of Spain. She was beautiful, intelligent and fun-loving. For nearly 20 years she and Henry made the perfect royal couple. She bore several children, but only Mary survived. Henry sought to have their marriage annulled, saying it was an unlawful union. The matter eventually led to the break with the Church of Rome. The divorce was finalised in 1533 and Catherine was banished from court. She died alone on 7th January 1536; a sad end to a glittering reign.

THE LAST PAPAL LEGATE

The seal of Cardinal Lorenzo Campeggio (the last papal legate to officiate in England). He referred Henry's application for an annulment directly to the Pope.

BORN TO BE QUEEN

Catherine was betrothed to Prince Arthur when only three to form an Anglo-Spanish alliance. They married in 1501 but within six months she was widowed. She was afterwards betrothed to Henry, who had always liked her, and when they married in 1509 it was out of genuine love.

CATHERINE'S DEFENCE

After much deliberation Catherine's, tribunal in front of the cardinals to contest Henry's application for a divorce, began on 18th June 1529. She argued convincingly that her marriage to Arthur was unconsummated so her union with Henry must be legal.

PERSONAL HYGIENE

Catherine was very particular about her personal hygiene. This very comfortable bathroom, with its fire and linen-lined tub, is very typical of those in the royal palaces.

PRINCESS MARY

Mary was the only child of Catherine and Henry to survive. Born on 18th February 1516 she was largely ignored by Henry after his divorce from Catherine, when her rights to the throne were nullified by Parliament. She was later crowned queen as Mary I in 1553.

CATHERINE'S MISSAL

Catherine was devoutly religious and had her own personal missal, richly bound in leather, which she took to mass to follow the prayers.

PATRON OF THE ARTS

Although usually regarded as a strong, powerful leader, not to say tyrannical in the latter years of his reign, Henry VIII had a gentler side to his nature. He was something of a patron of the arts. He liked to surround himself with beautiful objects and commissioned many paintings, statues and wood carvings. He furnished his many palaces sumptuously and acquired many exquisite pieces of jewellery and fine art, such as clocks. Hans Holbein, a German portrait painter, was employed to record the royal family for posterity. Henry set a precedent, and something of a new fashion at court, by composing musical tunes and setting verses to them.

DEVOUTLY RELIGIOUS

Henry was a surprisingly devout Catholic and was familiar with many religious writings. This illustration, from Henry's own psalter (book of psalms) shows the king reading liturgical texts, some of which he set to music.

COURTLY MUSIC

Professional musicians were employed to entertain the king at court and accompany him on his travels. Musicians nearly always performed in private, seldom at public functions, except dances. This lute, an early forerunner of the guitar, and flute are typical Tudor instruments.

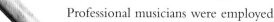

A MAN OF LETTERS

Henry was an accomplished scholar, though he found writing somewhat tedious. He dictated most of his official letters, but his private correspondence, and his poetry, he wrote himself. His personal writing box is shown here, decorated with the royal coat-of-arms. It was made in 1525 of painted wood and gilt leather.

AN ACCOMPLISHED MUSICIAN

Henry was himself an accomplished musician and is reputed to have had a good singing voice. He is also credited with writing a number of songs, including 'Pastance With Good Company' and possibly the words to 'Greensleeves'.

AN AVID READER

Henry was an avid reader and could converse in English, Spanish, French and Latin. He encouraged others to read and insisted that his children were well-versed in the art at an early age.

VIRTUOSO PERFORMANCE

Women were allowed few privileges at court, though Henry allowed any who were accomplished musicians to give private recitals. The woman in this picture is playing an early form of fiddle; note the shape of the bow.

EVENTS OF HENRY'S LIFE

~1527 22ND JUNE~
Henry starts divorce against Catherine of Aragon

~1528~
Cardinal Wolsey gives Hampton Court to Henry

~1529 18TH JUNE~
Catherine of Aragon starts her defence

~1530 29TH NOVEMBER~
Wolsey arrested, later dies

~1532~
Archbishop Warham dies. Thomas Cranmer becomes Archbishop of Canterbury. Act of Succession passed

~17TH MAY~
Thomas More resigns as Chancellor

BREAK WITH THE CHURCH OF ROME

There was already a growing body of people who objected to, and protested against corruption within the Catholic Church. They came to be known as Protestants and seized upon the opportunity to establish a new church in England by siding with the king. When the Pope refused to annul his marriage to Catherine of Aragon, Henry determined to take away the power of the clergy by Act of Parliament. Henry remained a Catholic throughout his life. The conversion of the Church of England to Protestantism came later, in Elizabeth I's reign.

HENRY DEFIES THE POPE

This contemporary woodcut (c.1538) depicting the Pope as an antichrist, shows Henry defying papal power. It is typical of the anti-Catholic feeling that swept Europe in the 16th century.

THE REFORMATION

In 1533 Parliament passed the Act of Appeals, asserting England's independence from Rome. The following year the Act of Supremacy made Henry 'Supreme Head of the Church of England'.

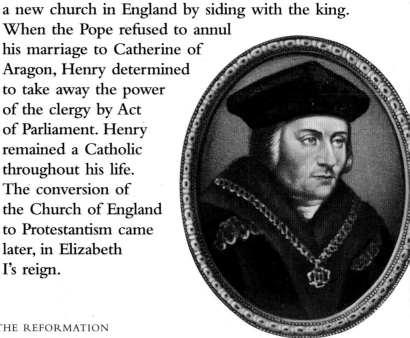

THE ARREST OF THOMAS MORE

Sir Thomas More, Lord Chancellor and chief minister at the time, was a devout Catholic and refused to acknowledge Henry as head of the English Church. He was arrested and executed in 1535.

DEFENDER OF THE FAITH

Ironically, in 1521 Henry wrote a book defending the Catholic faith against the Protestant writings of Martin Luther, earning him the title 'Defender of the Faith' from the Pope. The abbreviation F.D. still appears on coins today.

EVENTS OF HENRY'S LIFE

~1533~
Act of Appeals passed

~25TH JANUARY~
Henry secretly marries Anne Boleyn

WILLIAM WARHAM

Archbishop of Canterbury from 1504 to 1532, Warham had officiated at the marriage of Henry and Catherine. He fought against Henry's break with the Church of Rome all his life.

DEFENDING THE REALM

CANNON FIRE

Detail of a
bronze demi
cannon, found
aboard the
Mary Rose.
All Henry's
guns carried
the royal device
of a rose
in relief.

*H*enry VIII was a flamboyant and ambitious man, personally and politically. He took part in several military campaigns to strengthen his position in Europe, with varying degrees of success. Charles V of Spain, and Holy Roman Emperor, was also Catherine of Aragon's nephew and had already successfully attacked Rome, making the Pope politically subject to him. When Henry later sought permission of the Pope to divorce Catherine he was never likely to be received favourably. Following Henry's split with the Church of Rome, he spent the last years of his reign under threat of invasion to re-establish papal authority. In response, Henry built a chain of fortifications to protect the south coast.

THE ENGLISH NAVY

Although founded by his father, it was Henry VIII who first developed the navy into a proper fighting force. By the end of his reign the fleet was 80 strong.

BASTIONS OF DEFENCE

Deal Castle, Kent, as it appeared when newly completed in 1540. The largest of the Henrician coastal forts, it was also the most powerful, defended by cannons and handguns in three tiers of heavy bastions.

HENRY'S SOUTH COAST FORTIFICATIONS

This map shows the distribution of Henry's castle-building programme along the south coast, always vulnerable to attack from Spain and France. The defences were mostly built between 1538-40 with money and materials from the recently closed monasteries.

St. Ives
Falmouth
Falmouth
St. Mawes
Pendennis
Plymouth
Plymouth
Paignton
Teignmouth
Torquay
Dartmouth
Exmouth
Falmouth

FORTRESS PALACE

The only royal palace to be heavily fortified, the Tower of London, dating from Norman times, was a formidable fortress guarding Henry's capital city.

MEN–AT–ARMS

Tudor soldiers were only lightly armoured with helmets and breastplates (similar to this illustration). They were expected to provide their own weapons, which might be pistols, muskets, pikestaffs, or even crossbows.

EVENTS OF HENRY'S LIFE

~1533 23RD MAY~
Henry 'officially' divorces Catherine of Aragon

~7TH SEPTEMBER~
Princess Elizabeth born

~1534~
Act of Supremacy passed

~12TH APRIL~
Maid of Kent executed

~1535 22ND JUNE~
Bishop John Fisher executed

~6TH JULY~
Thomas More executed

🏰 *Henrician Castles*
🏰 *Henrician Blockhouses*
✿ *Other Forts & Castles*
● *Towns*

London
Greenwich
Tilbury
Gravesend
Chatham
Queenborough
Finsbury
Ness
Sheerness
Margate
Sandwich
Deal
Walmer
Dover
Folkstone
Sandgate
Hythe
Romney
Rye
Camber
Winchelsea
Hastings
Pevensey
Eastbourne
Bexhill
Beachy Head
Bodiam
Brighton
Bognor
Worthing
Chichester
Portsmouth
Southampton
Fort Brockhurst
Calshot
Fort Nelson
Portchester
Southsea
Cowes
Sandown
Carisbrooke
Yarmouth
Hurst
Bournemouth
Christchurch
Poole
Swanage
Sandsfoot
Portland

ANNE BOLEYN

BORN
1502

MARRIED
1533

DIVORCED
1536

EXECUTED
1536

When it became clear that Catherine was not going to bear Henry a son, he began to lose interest in her, especially as the queen's looks began to fade. He had a series of mistresses, amongst whom was Anne Boleyn. He developed a genuine love for her and they married, in secret, probably on 25th January 1533, four months before his divorce from Catherine was finalised. Having failed, like Catherine, to deliver the king a son and heir, Henry resolved to end his second marriage. He began to tire of Anne and accused her of adultery with, amongst others, her own brother George, and of plotting to murder him. One of the accused confessed under torture, condemning them all to death. For some reason Henry had the marriage annulled two days before her execution on 19th May 1536.

SIGN OF THE TIMES

The date of Anne's birth is unknown, but is usually given as 1502. Not a classically beautiful woman, she had six fingers on one hand, which Henry cited against her in the divorce as a sign of witchcraft.

WAITING TO DIE

On 24th April 1536 Anne's own uncle, the Duke of Norfolk, was appointed by Thomas Cromwell to gather evidence against her. Whilst imprisoned in the Tower of London she etched her signature into the wall of her cell.

THE FUTURE QUEEN

Anne gave birth to Elizabeth on 7th September 1533, just eight months after her 'official' marriage to Henry. Elizabeth was a great disappointment to Henry, but eventually became queen in 1558.

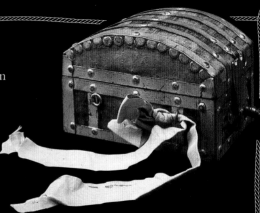

ANNE'S JEWEL BOX

Amongst Anne's most treasured possessions was her jewellery, which she carried in this charming casket on her frequent processions between royal palaces. It is on display at Leeds Castle, Kent, one of her favourite homes.

CHILDHOOD HOME

Henry courted Anne at Hever Castle, Kent, her family home, built in 1340 and extended by her father, Sir Thomas Bullen (or Boleyn). Her ghost is said to haunt the gardens of Hever each Christmas.

EXECUTIONER'S SWORD

Anne was taken to the scaffold on Tower Green a little before noon, wearing a robe of black damask. An executioner, skilled in the use of the sword, was brought over specially from France, at her request. A sword similar to this may have been used.

MARY BOLEYN

Mary Boleyn, Anne's elder sister, became Henry's mistress in 1521 and is rumoured to have borne him a son. Anne was made Queen Catherine's lady-in-waiting and soon aroused the king's interest in place of Mary.

THE ROYAL PALACES

TUDOR
KITCHENS

The kitchens at
Hampton Court
are still very much
as they were in
Henry's day.

*H*enry VIII spent a vast fortune on his royal residences, embellishing existing palaces and building some entirely new ones on a scale unprecedented by any other English monarch. He was determined to make an outward display of his wealth and power to all the figureheads of Europe. Henry's household regularly visited each of the palaces at different times of the year.

HAMPTON COURT PALACE

Hampton Court began as a small medieval manor, belonging to the Knights Hospitallers, a religious order. Greatly extended by Wolsey into a palace, he was forced to give it to Henry in 1528, who embellished it still further.

NONSUCH PALACE

In 1538 Henry began his most ambitious building project, the Palace of Nonsuch, in Surrey. It was to be the most magnificent palace in Europe, but was never completed. Today, all trace of it has gone.

GREENWICH PALACE

The Tudor palace of Placentia, birthplace of Henry VIII and Elizabeth I, stood by the Thames at Greenwich, then just a village outside London. It was a magnificent medieval palace, greatly extended by Henry, and was his favourite residence. Although rebuilt by Charles II to designs by Wren, this view by Canaletto (c.1750) of the buildings (later converted for use as a naval hospital, college and maritime museum) still give a good idea of the grandeur of the riverside setting.

JANE SEYMOUR

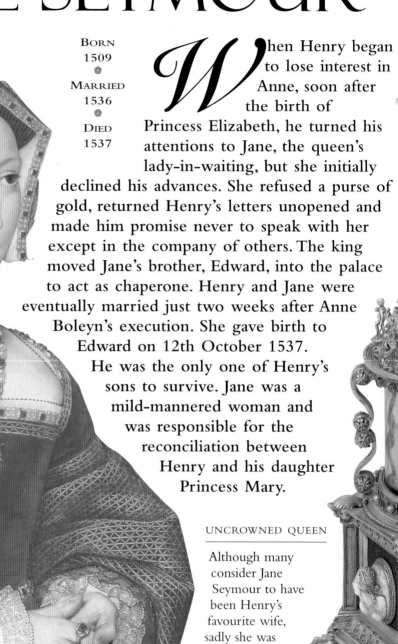

BORN
1509

MARRIED
1536

DIED
1537

*W*hen Henry began to lose interest in Anne, soon after the birth of Princess Elizabeth, he turned his attentions to Jane, the queen's lady-in-waiting, but she initially declined his advances. She refused a purse of gold, returned Henry's letters unopened and made him promise never to speak with her except in the company of others. The king moved Jane's brother, Edward, into the palace to act as chaperone. Henry and Jane were eventually married just two weeks after Anne Boleyn's execution. She gave birth to Edward on 12th October 1537. He was the only one of Henry's sons to survive. Jane was a mild-mannered woman and was responsible for the reconciliation between Henry and his daughter Princess Mary.

UNCROWNED QUEEN

Although many consider Jane Seymour to have been Henry's favourite wife, sadly she was never actually crowned queen before her untimely death on 24th October 1537.

THE FUTURE KING

As a young child Edward was intelligent and quite robust, but he was later struck down by a succession of illnesses. In January 1553 he contracted tuberculosis and died six months later, just 15 years old. He was the first king to be crowned as 'Supreme Head of the English Church'.

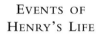

SALT OF THE EARTH

In medieval and Tudor times salt was considered a very expensive and important commodity, essential for the preservation of food. When Francis I, King of France, presented this combined clock and salt cellar, made of exquisitely wrought silver gilt, to Henry it would have been considered a fine gift.

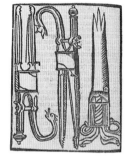

THE QUEEN DIES

Jane had a prolonged labour with Edward, finally giving birth by Caesarean section, the surgeons using implements similar to these. Complications set in and she died of blood poisoning two weeks later.

EVENTS OF HENRY'S LIFE

~1536~
Dissolution of monasteries begins

~7TH JANUARY~
Catherine of Aragon dies

~17TH MAY~
Henry divorces Anne Boleyn

THE KING MOURNS

Henry is said to have really loved Jane and was distraught when she died following the birth of Edward. Her body was laid to rest at Windsor, where he himself was later buried. She is the only wife to share his grave.

EUROPEAN RELATIONS

*W*hen Henry came to the throne England was still considered a minor player on the European political stage. Being a proud and arrogant man, he was keen to show his prowess on the battlefield and took part in several minor campaigns, with mixed results. In 1513 he joined forces with the Emperor Maximilian against France. When Wolsey's contrivances to hold the balance of power in Europe failed, it left Henry alone and humiliated. Wolsey was arrested in 1530 but died en-route to the Tower.

WRESTLING

Henry VIII loved to wrestle, but he was thrown to the floor by Francis I in their friendly contest.

THE FIELD OF THE CLOTH OF GOLD (1520)

Following several years of wars, an uneasy peace prevailed in which
Henry briefly held the balance of power between France and
Spain. Wolsey organised a meeting, full of pomp and pageantry,
with Francis I (of France) outside Calais to try and bring about a
permanent alliance. No expense was spared by Henry. A small
'town' of tents and pavilions was set up to house the two kings and
their retainers. Henry wore a gold cloak and the meeting came to
be known as 'The Field of the Cloth of Gold'.

EVENTS OF HENRY'S LIFE

~1536 19TH MAY~
Henry executes
Anne Boleyn

~MAY~
Henry marries
Jane Seymour

~8TH OCTOBER~
Pilgrimage of
Grace begins

~1537 FEBRUARY~
Robert Aske
executed

~12TH
OCTOBER~
Prince
Edward
born

SIEGE OF BOULOGNE

This woodcut
shows Henry's army
laying siege to
Boulogne in 1544,
in a later campaign.
Powerful cannons
break through the
walls, while armed
knights await the
opportunity to
rout the city.

THOMAS WOLSEY (1475-1530)

Cardinal Wolsey, although
of humble birth, was made
Chancellor by Henry in 1514.
He was a powerful
politician who
virtually governed
the country
single-handedly
for 15 years,
until he fell from
favour in 1529.

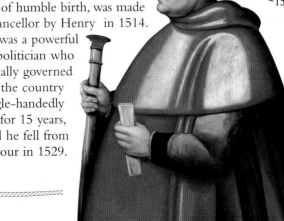

ANNE OF CLEVES

BORN
1515
•
MARRIED
1540
•
DIVORCED
1540
•
DIED
1557

*H*enry seems to have genuinely grieved for Jane Seymour and did not remarry for over two years following her death. Until then, Henry had married the women of his own choice, unusual for the monarchy who usually married for the benefits of political alliance. Thomas Cromwell and several other of the king's ministers were becoming increasingly concerned about Henry's role in Europe and were keen for the king to make a marriage of alliance to strengthen his position. Charles V of Spain and Francis I were mustering an army against England, threatening to re-establish papal power, so Henry desperately needed an ally in Europe. Somewhat reluctantly, he agreed to a political marriage of convenience, even though the threat of invasion passed.

IMMEDIATE DIVORCE

The marriage was never consummated and Henry sought an immediate divorce, which was granted six months later.

MATCHMAKER

Thomas Cromwell, Henry's current chief minister, was entrusted with the task of finding the king a new wife. A convenient political alliance between England and Germany might be formed if he could persuade Henry to marry one of the Duke of Cleves' sisters.

A COMFORTABLE RETIREMENT

Henry and Anne were a disappointment to one another from the start. She could speak no English and had few social graces. Educated more in domestic skills than in art, literature and music, all of which Henry loved, Anne retired to Richmond Palace, where she lived peaceably until her death in 1557.

THE 'FLANDERS MARE'

Holbein was sent to Germany to paint portraits of Anne and her sister Amelia. Henry chose Anne and agreed to marry her on the strength of it, but was later very disappointed with her, calling her the 'Flanders Mare'.

EVENTS OF HENRY'S LIFE

~1537 24TH OCTOBER~
Jane Seymour dies

~1538~
Henry builds Nonsuch Palace

~1540~
Last monastery closes

~6TH JANUARY~
Henry marries Anne of Cleves

~JULY~
Thomas Cromwell executed

~12TH JULY~
Henry divorces Anne of Cleves

DISSOLUTION OF THE MONASTERIES

*I*n Henry's time there were about 850 monasteries in England and Wales, housing about 9000 monks and nuns. Many of their traditional duties, such as writing books and healing the sick, had been taken over by professional people and standards had indeed slipped, but most of the charges levelled against them were false or exaggerated. As the new head of the Church, Henry saw his chance to close the monasteries down and seize their wealth. Thomas Cromwell was responsible for 'dissolving', or closing the monasteries between 1536–40.

REUSED STONE

In addition to topping up Henry's coffers by claiming their lands and riches, the monasteries also served as convenient quarries for stone in his castle-building programme, as shown above.

'PILGRIMS OF GRACE'

Robert Aske led a pilgrimage from Yorkshire to London to demand that Henry reopen the monasteries. They disbanded peaceably but Henry treacherously executed Aske and many of his followers.

A TYPICAL DAY IN A MONASTERY	
Midnight	Matins (church service)
1am	Retire to bed
5am	Prime (church service)
6am	Breakfast
7am	Work duties
9am	Chapter Mass (church service)
10am	Meeting with abbot
11am	High Mass (church service)
12 noon	Dinner
1pm	Rest in dormitory
2pm	Work duties
4pm	Vespers (church service)
5pm	Work duties
6pm	Supper
7pm	Evening Prayer
8pm	Retire to bed

PENALTY FOR RESISTANCE

Cromwell's officials visited each monastery and requested that the brethren close it down voluntarily, forfeiting all their land and possessions to the king. Most complied, but if they refused they faced imprisonment, torture and possible execution, usually on trumped-up charges.

FALLEN FROM GRACE

One of the largely unproven charges levelled against the monasteries was that the monks and nuns had sunken into debauchery, spending their time drinking and fraternising instead of in quiet prayer.

AFTER THE DISSOLUTION

Many of the richer monasteries were sold or let to the king's favourites, who might convert them into fine houses. Others, like Bayham Abbey, Sussex, were stripped of their riches and left to slowly fall into ruins.

EVENTS OF HENRY'S LIFE

~1540 28TH JULY~
Henry marries
Catherine Howard

~1542~
Battle of Solway Moss

~13TH FEBRUARY~
Catherine Howard
executed

~1543 12TH JULY~
Henry marries
Catherine Parr

~1544 18TH
SEPTEMBER~
Siege of
Boulogne

~1545
19TH JULY~
*Mary
Rose*
sinks

CATHERINE HOWARD

BORN
1521

MARRIED
1540

EXECUTED
1542

UNSEEMLY BEHAVIOUR

Catherine was accused of adultery and conduct unbecoming a queen by Archbishop Cranmer. She was tried and found guilty, and later beheaded on 13th February 1542.

Catherine Howard became another pawn in the power struggles of Henry's court. Henry's marriage to Anne of Cleves had been a disaster and he soon began to look for a new bride. Anne's charming lady-in-waiting, Catherine Howard, soon caught his attention. Thomas Cromwell had strongly supported the king's marriage to Anne and his enemies were quick to encourage Henry to divorce her and marry Catherine as a means of ousting him from power. They married on 28th July 1540 just 16 days after Henry's divorce.

THE QUEEN'S LAST JOURNEY

This is the last view Catherine Howard would have seen, before her imprisonment, as she approached the Traitor's Gate at the Tower of London. Her only real crime was in having a flirtatious nature, for which she paid with her life.

TRAITOR'S GATE

Traitor's Gate at the Tower of London (formerly known as the Water Gate) so called because it is where prisoners arriving by boat were admitted to the Tower. Catherine was taken there by royal barge from Hampton Court for imprisonment and trial.

ÆTATIS   SVÆ·21

RESTLESS SPIRIT

Like Anne Boleyn, her cousin, also executed by Henry, Catherine Howard's spirit seems unable to rest. Her ghost is said to haunt this gallery at Hampton Court Palace.

FLIRTATIOUS NATURE

Catherine Howard was the niece of the Duke of Norfolk. She became lady-in-waiting to Anne of Cleves at just 19. She was high spirited and quite uninhibited which, tragically for her, aroused the interest of the king.

CATHERINE PARR

BORN
1512
•
MARRIED
1543
•
DIED
1548

Catherine Parr was the daughter of a minor noble, Sir Thomas Parr, who had risen through the ranks of Henry's court to become Controller of the Royal Household. Very little is known about Catherine's early life, or her courtship with Henry. A mature woman of 31 when she married Henry on 12th July 1543, she was already twice widowed. Well educated, she brought a sense of calm and dignity to the royal court. Henry was by now suffering from many ailments and Catherine nursed him in his final years. She supervised Edward's education and reconciled Mary and Elizabeth with Henry.

PRESENT FROM AN EMPEROR

This grotesque parade helmet was given to Henry by the Emperor Maximilian I in about 1514. By the time he married Catherine Parr his face had become so bloated the helmet no longer fitted.

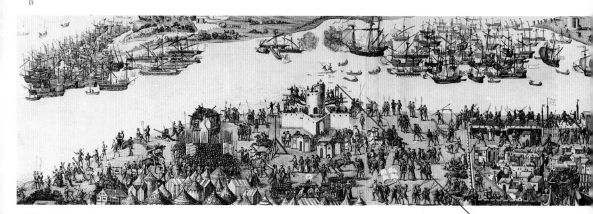

INSPECTING THE FLEET

Henry visited Portsmouth in July 1545 to inspect his navy in Southampton Water. He watched, humiliated, as the *Mary Rose* sank before his eyes.

This is where the *Mary Rose* sank, which is marked in the picture by floating bodies.

THE *MARY ROSE*

Henry's flagship, the *Mary Rose* (built in 1509), sank in the Solent on 19th July 1545. It was the first ship to be fitted with broadside-firing guns.

THE KING'S GREAT BED

Henry slept alone in the last years of his life in a bed similar to this one and had become so gross and overweight that he had to be hoisted into and out of bed by ropes and pulleys.

RELICS OF THE PAST

This fine collection of pewter plates was recovered from the *Mary Rose*. The wreck, and many artefacts of everyday life in Tudor times, are now on display in Portsmouth Historic Dockyard.

THE QUEEN LIVES !

Catherine Parr outlived Henry, even though she was unable to bear him any children. A little while after the king's death she married Thomas Seymour, but died in 1548 after giving birth to a girl.

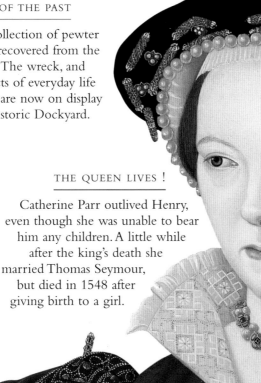

THE FADING YEARS

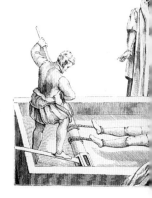

*T*he sad, lonely figure that Henry had become by 1547 was a far cry from the strapping, athletic young man who ascended the throne some 38 years before. Always prone to severe headaches, which caused him to rage frequently, he also suffered bouts of smallpox and malaria. Both his legs were severely ulcerated, whether as a result of syphilis (probably also responsible for his fertility problems), varicose veins, which thrombosed, or osteomyelitis (a chronic infection, possibly caused by a jousting accident) is uncertain. The ulcers turned gangrenous and the smell of rotting flesh accompanied him in his final years. When Henry died on 28th January 1547 at St. James's Palace, few mourned the passing of his reign of tyranny.

REIGN OF A TYRANT

Towards the end of his reign, Henry became more and more tyrannical in removing from office anyone who opposed him. Many thousands were tortured or executed by his order.

PRIVATE HEALTH CARE

In the final years of his life Henry required constant medical attention. This instrument case, decorated with the royal arms, belonged to his personal barber surgeon.

POWER STRUGGLE

John Dudley, Duke of Northumberland, one of the Council of Regency appointed by Henry to govern during Edward's minority. He later schemed to place Lady Jane Grey, his daughter-in-law, on the throne instead of Mary.

SAFETY FIRST

The king became obsessed with his personal safety in later life. He carried his own private lock when travelling, which he attached to his bed chamber door. Whilst staying at Allington Castle he went so far as to have himself walled-in each night!

A WEIGHT PROBLEM

By the end of his life Henry had become quite obese and disfigured by illness. He had to be carried everywhere by servants and lifted up and down stairs with a hoist.

A GLOSSARY OF INTERESTING HENRICIAN TERMS

Arrogant - The word arrogant, in the sense of being proud and assertive, is derived from Catherine of Aragon, who remained dignified throughout the long ordeal of her trial and divorce from Henry.

Benevolence - The modern meaning of this word is to act in a kindly manner, but in Tudor times it was a 'voluntary' tax given to the government in the form of a loan.

Limelight - The modern word means to be in the glare of publicity, but it has its origins in the Tudor theatre. Following Henry VIII's break with Rome, much of the colour and pageantry went from people's lives. Popular theatre helped fill the void. There is evidence to suggest that a technique of burning lime to create a bright light, to illuminate the stage, was developed in the 16th century.

Scotland Yard - The famous headquarters of the London Metropolitan Police Force acquired its unusual name from Henry's palace at Whitehall. Visiting royalty from Scotland stayed in a special suite of rooms, with gardens, which came to be known as 'Scotland Yard', which once stood on the site.

Sewer - The word sewer originally meant a drainage ditch to collect excess water from the land. In towns many people threw their effluent into these ditches, causing them to smell. Eventually they were enclosed within pipes, hence the modern use of the word.

Subsidy - Nowadays a subsidy is usually a grant of money given by the government to a taxpayer, but in Henry's day it was a tax levied by the government according to the extent of a person's landholdings or goods.

ACKNOWLEDGEMENTS

Addax would like to thank: Tim Feeley, Graham Rich, Tracey Pennington and Peter Done for their assistance.

Copyright © 1995 Addax Retail Publishing Ltd.

First published in Great Britain by Addax Retail Publishing Ltd., Great Britain. All rights reserved.
No part of this publication may be reproduced, stored in a retrieval system, or transmitted in any form or by any means, electronic, mechanical, photocopying, recording or otherwise, without prior written permission of the copyright owner.

Acknowledgements: Picture Credits t=top, b=bottom, c=centre, l=left, r=right
Abbreviations : BAL = Bridgeman Art Library, London
Ann Ronan at Image Select; 3br, 4cr,4/5c. Board of Trustees of the National Museums and Galleries on Merseyside (Walker Art Gallery, Liverpool); OFCc/4bl. The Board of Trustees of the Royal Armouries; OBCbl/2tl, OBCtr/5c, OFCr/28tl. British Library, London/BAL; OBCtl/8tl, 9ct, OBCbc/25c. Crown Copyright/Historic Royal Palaces; 20tl, 27tl, 27c. David Sellman; 15cl. English Heritage Photographic Library; 12bl, 24cl. Fitzwilliam Museum, University of Cambridge/BAL; 22/23ct. Forbes Magazine Collection, New York/BAL; IFC/1. Fotomas Index; 16b. Harrogate Museums and Art Gallery, North Yorkshire/BAL; 7tr. Heather Angel; 2/3cb. Hever Castle Ltd; OFCbl/8/9c, 30/31ct. Hever Castle Ltd/BAL; 14l, 15br, 23cb. Hulton Deutsch Collection Ltd; OBCcl/6tr, 30tl. John Bethell/BAL; 20/21ct. Kunsthistorisches Museum, Vienna/BAL; OFCcl/18l. © Leeds Castle Foundation; 4/5ct, 6/7cb, 7cl, 15tr. Louvre, Paris/Giraudon/BAL; OFCbr/11. The Mansell Collection; 25tl. Mary Evans Picture Library; 4/5b, 6l, 9br, 10tl, 10bl/32, 10cr, 12/13ct, 14/15cb, 19br, 21tr, 22bl, 24bl. © Mary Rose Trust; 8bl, 9c, OBCc/10/11ct, 12tl, 28cr. National Maritime Museum, Greenwich; 3ct, 13cr, OFCtr/13r, 15tl, 20/21, 22cr. The National Portrait Gallery, London; 7br, 17br, OBCcr/27tr, 29br, 31br. © Portsmouth City Council; 28b. Private Collection/BAL; 26/27, 29tl. Reproduced by kind permission of the President and Council of the Royal College of Surgeons of London; 19c. The Royal Collection © Her Majesty The Queen; 17t. Victoria & Albert Museum, London; 29c. Victoria & Albert Museum, London/BAL; 2tr, 8bl, 16tl. The Worshipful Company of Barbers; 30bl. Worshipful Company of Goldsmiths; 18/19c.

Every effort has been made to trace the copyright holders and we apologise in advance for any unintentional omissions.
We would be pleased to insert the appropriate acknowledgement in any subsequent edition of this publication.

A CIP Catalogue for this book is available from the British Library. ISBN 1 86007 030 2